Stoats and Weasels

A curious stoat pops up its head

Stoats and Weasels

John Reynolds

Priory Press Limited

Young Naturalist Books

Foxes
Squirrels
Bats
Snakes and Lizards
Frogs and Toads
Hedgehogs
Badgers
Deer
Rabbits and Hares
Spiders
Otters
Rats and Mice
Stoats and Weasels
Bees and Wasps
Birds of Prey
Ants
Beetles
Pond Life
Crickets and Grasshoppers

SBN 85078 190 6
Copyright © 1974 Priory Press Ltd
2nd impression, 1976
First published by Priory Press Ltd
49, Lansdowne Place, Hove, Sussex BN3 1HS
Filmset by Keyspools Ltd, Golborne, Lancs
Printed in Great Britain at
The Pitman Press, Bath

Contents

A weasel

1 : Terror in the Countryside

Lolloping towards us as we walk along the woodland track we see a rabbit. It seems curiously unafraid. We stand perfectly still. It approaches quite slowly, zigzagging a little, and passes right by us without even noticing that we are there. As it passes we see that its eyes are glazed and bulging. It seems to be in a trance.

We remain frozen to the spot, like blocks of stone, and have not long to wait. Bounding along the track towards us, and obviously on the trail of the rabbit, comes a stoat. It is an extraordinarily thin animal, like a length of rope, and it is not half the size of the rabbit. It leaps along, with arched back, for a few yards, then stops to look around. It is in no great hurry, although it is hunting its next meal. It raises its head, sniffing the scent of the rabbit, and then moves on again. If we do not move it fails to see us, just as the rabbit did. It has its mind on business.

If we are in the wood ten or fifteen minutes later we may hear a wild squeal, as the stoat catches up with and kills its prey.

When we thought that the rabbit appeared to be in a

7

Stoats are thin and lithe enough to follow rabbits down their holes and catch them there.

trance it was not our imagination. Rabbits pursued by stoats do behave that way. Some people have thought that the stoat, catching the rabbit by surprise, gets in an early nip behind the ears which produces a kind of paralysis in the rabbit, but there is no real evidence of this. It seems that the rabbit is simply scared stiff. It knows that there is no escape. Although over a short distance it can run faster than the stoat, the stoat does not worry. It is prepared to follow the rabbit for hours. With its acute senses of scent, hearing and sight, it never loses the trail and it never loses patience. Watching the last phases of the chase is like watching a moving picture in slow motion. The rabbit plods along, hopelessly, with the stoat trotting un-

A weasel drags its prey, a wood mouse, off to eat.

hurriedly behind it. Eventually the rabbit stops and starts to squeal before the stoat even touches it.

The stoat is one of the small carnivorous animals which are the terror of the countryside. It is intensely fierce, brave and bloodthirsty. No living creature is really safe from it. It can climb. It can follow its prey into their burrows. It can also swim well. The weasel, a near relation of the stoat, is so small that it can crawl into mouse holes.

Although they are such savage killers, stoats and weasels are attractive animals to watch. Like most carnivorous animals, they are fond of play. Romping about and chasing each other helps to keep them fit for the more serious business of life. Young stoats, which are called *kittens*, will play for hours. And adult stoats often join in.

Stoats may play on their own or in a group of as many as fifteen. When several are playing together they chase each other, box and wrestle, turn somersaults and leap several feet into the air.

They would be very attractive pets if they could be trusted with other animals. They can give a human being quite a nasty bite. Weasels, being tinier, are less dangerous, though just as bloodthirsty. It is said that they can be easily tamed and even allowed the run of the house. But even they can give a person a sharp nip.

An American long-tailed weasel. Like the European stoat, the end of its tail is dark.

2 : Stoats and Weasels in the World

Wherever small rodents and other small animals live, there we shall find stoats and weasels to eat them. There are about 70 different kinds of stoats, weasels and animals like them in the world. Their scientific name is *Mustelidae*, which is a useful word to remember, because some of them are not known as stoats or weasels at all.

The stoats and weasels which live in Britain are northern animals. They are found in Europe, Asia and America in the temperate zone and right up into the forests on the edge of the Arctic. In America the stoat is known as the *short-tailed weasel*. There is also in America a *long-tailed weasel* – because, of course, it has a long tail. Another American member of the stoat family is the *black-footed weasel*. In Europe an animal even smaller than the British weasel, and known as the *least weasel*, is found. Strangely, no weasels are found in Ireland, and stoats are uncommon there.

Another group of *Mustelidae* animals are the martens. Britain has one of them, the *pine marten*, though it is un-common. It is found chiefly in wooded mountain regions

Above: *A ferret. Farmers used to have ferrets to keep down the rabbits.* Opposite: *A beech marten peers out of a hollow tree.*

like the Lake District, central Wales and north-west Scotland. A rather similar animal, the *beech marten*, lives in southern and central Europe. The *American marten*, which is also very like the others, is much valued for its fur. Another of the tribe, the *Himalayan marten*, lives in the mountains of China, Burma and India. A large marten, which also lives in America, is for some strange reason known as the *fisher*, although it does not live on fish. All the martens spend most of their time in trees, though they can run very fast on the ground and are also excellent swimmers.

If you have ever visited an old-fashioned farm you may have seen a *ferret*. It is like a stoat, only larger. Most ferrets

kept in captivity are albinos: they have white (or creamy-white) fur and pink eyes. Some, however, have dark brown fur, with lighter underparts. These are known as *polecat ferrets*. There is almost no difference between them and wild *polecats*, which are still found in Britain. They are rare now but survive in mountain country, especially in Wales. Ferrets were formerly kept on most farms, to help in catching rabbits. They were put into rabbit holes to drive the rabbits out. Now that rabbits are scarce, however, there is not much work for ferrets to do, so few farms have them.

An animal which has become wild in Britain in recent years is the *mink*. It is an American animal, like a stoat but

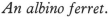

An albino ferret.

A polecat. They are still wild in the less populated parts of Britain and Europe.

bigger, which was bred for the sake of its fur. Mink coats are very expensive. From about 1930 onwards mink began to escape from mink farms which had been started in Britain. Now there are many of them breeding by streams and lakes in Wales, south-west England and perhaps in Scotland.

Even more precious than mink is the fur of a Siberian animal known as the *sable*. It has been hunted for its fur so much that it is now scarce, but it is now protected by law.

A handsome member of the *Mustelidae* is the *striped skunk*, which lives in America. It is beautifully striped in black and white and has a splendid bushy tail. But it can squirt from its glands a fluid with the most horrible smell,

15

Above: *The skunk, well known for the nasty smells it can make.*
Below: *the South American grison.*

The yellow-throated marten, from the forests of Asia.

and it uses this as a defence. Other animals, including men, have learned to leave the skunk well alone. Several other kinds of skunk are also found in America, including one, the *hooded skunk*, which lives as far south as sub-tropical Mexico.

South America has the *tayra*, an animal which, like the martens, lives mainly in trees. Where the forests give way to plains, in Argentina and other countries nearby, the tayra is replaced by the *grison*, or *huron*, and by several kinds of skunk.

Over in Africa are found the *zorilla*, an animal like the polecat but decorated with bold black-and-white stripes.

17

A civet. The civets are in the same family as the stoats, weasels and martens.

There are also several African weasels. The tropical forests of Asia have the *yellow-throated marten* to chase its squirrels and mice among the trees. Here and in Africa, however, the place of the stoats and weasels is taken mainly by a related group of animals known as the *civets*.

In general, therefore, the stoats and weasels mostly live in temperate and sub-polar regions. There are none in

Australia.

3: The Stoat

We have already noticed that the stoat is not nearly as big as the rabbits it often kills. The length of the male is about fourteen inches, of which four inches is tail. The female is much smaller. The stoat's body is long and slender. It has a long neck and a narrow head with a pointed nose. Its legs are short, and so are its little round ears. Although its eyes are bright, they are not particularly sharp. To know what is going on around it, it relies mostly on its nose and hearing.

In summer the stoat is reddish-brown. Its underparts, including its throat, are white or cream-coloured. In the north, including northern Britain, its coat usually turns white in winter. Sometimes you may also see a white or partly white stoat in southern England. One part of the stoat's fur, though, never turns white. That is the tip of its tail, which is always black.

White stoats have for many centuries been hunted for their fur, which is known as *ermine*. The stoats themselves are sometimes known as ermine, too. When they are dressed in their full finery, English judges and nobles wear

An early fall of snow has caught this stoat still in his summer coat, brown on top and white underneath.

ermine on their cloaks. You can see the snow-white trimmings with black flecks in them. The black flecks are the stoats' tails.

Besides being white, the stoat's winter coat is much thicker than its summer one, which, of course, is what makes the fur valuable. The stoat wears this white coat as camouflage in a snow-covered countryside. Unlike many northern animals, the stoat does not hibernate but stays awake and running about right through the winter.

The male stoat is known as a dog stoat; the female as a bitch stoat; but the young are, oddly enough, called kittens. The young are born in March or April. The den is in an old rabbit burrow or hollow tree, or a little cave among rocks or in a stone wall. Between four and nine young stoats are the usual number in a litter, and they are born blind and naked. For a long time they are suckled by their mother. Their eyes do not open until they are five or six weeks old, by which time they have also grown a coat of silvery fur. It is seven weeks or more before they venture outdoors with their mother and start to play.

A stoat in winter. His coat turns completely white except for the tip of his tail, which stays black.

Above: *Although they are small, stoats and weasels are extremely fierce.* Opposite: *In autumn the stoat's fur begins to change colour, and gets whiter and whiter.*

The breeding cycle of the stoat involves a curious process known as *delayed implantation*. Mating takes place in the weeks soon after the birth of the young, in the early summer. The fertilized eggs then stay in the mother's body, without growing, for many months. In fact, they do

23

not start to develop until the following spring, when the growth period before birth is three to four weeks.

Young stoats are grown up at the age of about two months. The young females therefore mate about June or July, but with them too the process of delayed implantation occurs, and the young are not born until the following spring.

When the young emerge from the nest the mother deliberately starts to educate them. She plays with them and shows them how to stalk and pounce. She cuffs them when they misbehave. All of them remain in a family group for months, sometimes for most of the winter. Occasionally several family groups join together and hunt in a pack.

Stoats, whether in families or singly, do not wander just anywhere in the countryside. They have their own beat or territory, which is usually on farmland because plenty of mice, voles and small birds are to be found there. Although we may possibly see them at any hour of the day, they do most of their hunting at night.

In Chapter I we read about the behaviour of a stoat on the trail of a rabbit. When it catches the rabbit it kills it with some sharp bites at the base of the ear. It starts to eat its prey at the same spot. So if, when walking in the countryside, we find a rabbit with the back of its head gnawed away we can be sure that a stoat (or weasel) has been around. Perhaps we have frightened it away and it is

24

Opposite: *Stoats are clever and quick but very inquisitive. They are always popping up to see what is going on.*

A stoat rolls playfully on wet moss after it has been raining.

still watching us, waiting for us to go away and allow it to finish its meal. Stoats need to keep killing in order to get enough to eat. A stoat needs to eat food about one third of its own weight each day. Supposing you weigh 100 pounds, if you were to eat at the same rate as the stoat you would get through a pile of food weighing over 30 pounds!

As well as showing extreme patience in following the trail of a rabbit for hours, the stoat has other methods of catching its prey. One of the most exciting it uses with birds. If it sees a flock of birds feeding on the ground in the open, it knows that they will probably fly away before it can catch one. So it moves cautiously into the open, at some distance from the birds, and starts to play with its tail. Faster and faster it spins around, leaping into the air, turning somersaults, like a professional acrobat. The birds stop feeding to watch the giddy performance. They become so fascinated that they do not notice that the stoat is getting nearer. Suddenly, when it judges it is close enough, the stoat gives a mighty leap and lands on top of the nearest bird.

We have mentioned rabbits and birds as prey for stoats, but the chief food of the stoat consists of rats, mice and voles. It will also catch and eat fish. And it loves eggs. If you are very lucky you may one day see a stoat rolling an egg away to eat it in comfort.

This stoat is examining a hen's egg before rolling it away to eat.

4: The Weasel

The weasel is very like a miniature stoat. The length of the male is about eight inches, with a tail two or three inches long. The female is much smaller. Apart from size, the main difference between stoats and weasels is in the colour of the tail. The stoat always has a black tip to its tail; the weasel never does. The weasel's coat is a rather brighter red-brown than the stoat's, and the underparts are whiter.

Weasels in Britain never change their colour to white in winter, though some of those which live in colder countries do. Male weasels are called dogs; females, bitches; and the young ones, kittens; just as with stoats.

The breeding habits of the weasel are, however, different from those of the stoat. There is no delayed implantation (see page 23). They mate in early spring. The gestation period, between mating and the birth of the young, is about 35 days, so April and May are the months when most young weasels are born. There is often, however, a second litter in August.

From four to eight young are born in each litter. They

A snow-bound weasel comes up for a quick look round.

are born blind and naked but mature more quickly than young stoats. Female weasels are very devoted mothers and will fight fiercely to defend their young. When the young leave the nest their mother trains them in the arts of stalking and killing, and, as with stoats, weasels often hunt together in family parties or packs.

Like stoats, too, weasels tend to stay in their own chosen territory. They can manage, however, with much less than stoats. A family of stoats will need up to 100 acres of land to hunt over, whereas a family of weasels will find about 10 acres enough.

A family of weasels. They nest in holes of all kinds, often taken over from other animals.

The weasel's body is so thin and agile that it can squeeze into tiny holes and cracks.

Like stoats, weasels are largely nocturnal, though they hunt more often than stoats by day as well. Their small size gives them an advantage over stoats because it lets them enter mouseholes. The body of the weasel is so slender and thin that if ever you see it sticking out of a mouse's hole you may easily think it is a snake for a moment. Weasels kill much of their prey underground. After killing and enjoying a feast, they often curl up in

A weasel pounces on an unlucky mouse.

their victim's hole and have a nap for a few hours. Like
stoats, they need to eat about a third of their weight in food
every day, so when they wake up they are very hungry and
need to start hunting again. When corn was stacked for the
winter in ricks a family of weasels would often move into
a rick in autumn and grow fat by eating the mice which
were eating the grain.

Weasels use the same tricks and tactics as stoats to

34

Weasels swim well—they are in the same family as otters—and enjoy a meal of fish.

Like all their kinsmen they are very curious. Here one reaches up on its hind legs to look over the grass.

catch their victims. Although so small, they can tackle a full-grown rabbit. They will also kill adult rats, which are fierce animals and have large sharp teeth with which to defend themselves. Weasels are incredibly brave, and a mother weasel will attack a man if he tries to interfere with her young ones.

Like stoats, weasels can climb and swim well. In streams they chase and kill water voles and eat baby moorhens and ducklings. In woods and hedges they climb trees and bushes to rob the nests of birds, eating both the eggs and the young birds. Nothing is safe from them.

When hunting and playing, young weasels have a shrill squeak or squeal. Adult weasels have a deeper voice – a kind of screaming bark, which they use when alarmed. Weasels have a habit of standing up on their hind legs from time to time, to survey the countryside. However, it is thought that they hunt chiefly by scent rather than sight.

Opposite: A stoat stands up on his hind legs to look round, showing its creamy white underparts. Below: You can see from this picture how small weasels are – not much bigger than a large leaf.

5: Their Enemies

Stoats and weasels are so strong and fierce that they have few enemies. Inexperienced hawks and owls will sometimes pounce on stoats and, more often, on smaller weasels. This often proves an expensive mistake for the bird of prey. A weasel has very loose skin and is sometimes able to wriggle around in the talons of its captor and bite it.

Large carnivorous animals generally leave stoats and weasels well alone. Not only can stoats and weasels fight back fiercely but they have little flesh on their thin, lithe, muscular bodies. Even more daunting, they have glands beneath their tails from which they can squirt an evil-smelling fluid. You have already read about the skunk's scent glands (see page 15). Most of the *Mustelidae* have similar glands, not as powerful as those of the skunk but quite enough to put any animal off its dinner.

Stoats and weasels therefore have only one serious enemy, but that is enough. It is man. A stoat or even a weasel can do so much damage in a poultry pen that this is understandable. When surrounded by a lot of squawking and defenceless hens and chickens a stoat or weasel will

39

Opposite: *Sometimes stoats and weasels are too inquisitive for their own good. They stick their heads out—and a farmer with a gun is waiting.*

often go berserk and kill far more birds than it needs to eat. Then it gets shot by an outraged farmer.

Gamekeepers, whose duty it is to protect and preserve pheasants, are even more deadly enemies. Pheasants and partridges live and nest out-of-doors, where they fall an easy prey to prowling stoats and weasels. So keepers shoot or trap them whenever they can. Many stoats too were often caught in traps set for rats and rabbits, before such traps were made illegal.

Both stoats and weasels have a habit which makes them an easy target for a man with a gun. They are enormously inquisitive. When danger threatens they bolt for the nearest cover, but within a few minutes their curiosity gets the better of them and they poke out their heads to find out what is happening. But the cunning keeper is waiting for them.

Because of constant persecution, stoats and weasels are much scarcer than once they were, though they are not in any danger of being exterminated. Weasels especially have found their way into towns, where they live in parks surrounded by houses. They are safe there, because no-one shoots them.

Within reason, stoats and weasels are useful animals to have on a farm, because of the enormous numbers of rats and mice they kill. In years when rats and mice are unusually numerous, which happens every now and then, the population of stoats and weasels generally increases

A swimming weasel.

too. The population of stoats and weasels dropped considerably when rabbits were almost wiped out by the epidemic of myxomatosis in the 1950s. So there is a close relationship between the numbers of stoats and weasels and the numbers of the animals on which they feed.

In Saxon times, a thousand or more years ago, weasels were often kept in houses as mouse-catchers. Cats were then either very scarce or unknown over much of England, and people had weasels instead. They were very good mousers, too.

Young weasels are not very difficult to tame, and they make attractive pets. They are extremely playful and love to romp around a room. They love, too, to be tickled. However, it is as well to remember that they can bite, and bite hard, and that they will do so instinctively if suddenly alarmed. If allowed the run of the house they can make a nuisance of themselves by being too inquisitive, poking their noses everywhere.

A polecat–one of the largest European members of the Mustelidae *family.*

6: Polecats and Martens

If ever you find yourself travelling along a country road in central or north Wales late at night you may be lucky enough to see a large animal on the road in front of you. You will probably be surprised and puzzled, because of its size. What British animal is there which is as large as a big cat or even a fox, with a fine bushy tail?

The animal is a polecat, and it looks larger than it really is because of its habit of fluffing out its long fur. Actually it is sixteen or eighteen inches long, with a tail of six or eight inches. It is dark brown – or rather the tips of its hairs are dark brown while the parts nearer the skin are pale buff. This gives the coat of the polecat a curious clouded colour. The underparts are dark, instead of being lighter as in most animals. Around its eyes and across its nose are some black markings, like a mask. Another black band runs across the forehead, from ear to ear. Apart from these black marks, the head and face of the polecat are creamy white. So the polecat is a handsome animal.

In build it is very like the stoat. It has a long, slender body and short legs; but its head is broader than the stoat's.

Opposite: *A polecat with its prey. Instead of being camouflaged polecats have bright markings which are meant to warn other animals: "I am dangerous! Keep away!"* Above: *A pair of adult polecats.*

Once common throughout most of Britain, the polecat has been almost exterminated because of the damage it does to poultry and game. It has a special fondness for domestic fowls, killing far more than it needs to eat. Unlike the stoat, it is not a good climber, but it can swim well. Polecats like wooded and hilly country, but in Wales they are often found in marshy valleys and along the sea coast.

45

They are expert at catching fish, including eels, and also frogs. Polecats have a curious habit of laying up a store of frogs for future use. They paralyse the frogs by a bite at the base of the skull and then stuff them into a hiding-place among rocks or in an old rabbit burrow. As many as several dozen have been found stowed away together in such a hoard. Polecats also eat rats, mice, birds and eggs, and can kill snakes. Most of their hunting is done at night, and they rely more on sound and scent than on sight.

Like stoats and weasels, the polecat often uses the

A nest of baby polecats about a week old.

burrows of other animals, especially rabbits. It can, however, dig its own burrows. Being an intelligent animal, it usually makes sure there is more than one entrance or exit, so that it has a way of escape. It also often digs a special chamber for sleeping.

In spring the female will take over one of these dormitory rooms for a nest. She lines it with grass and leaves until it forms a large ball, with one small opening. Here the young are born, usually in April or May. The polecat is not an animal in which delayed implantation (see page 23)

Ten-day-old ferrets. They will be strong enough to kill a fully-grown rabbit at eight weeks, and will eat a pound of meat a day between them.

occurs; it has a gestation period of six or seven weeks, so for spring litters mating takes place in February. Often there are second litters in late summer.

The litters consist of four to eight young, born blind and naked. Their eyes open at about fourteen days. Although mother polecats educate their young, as stoats and weasels do, the family does not stick together and hunt in packs when the young are mature. Instead each polecat goes off and hunts on its own.

Like most other *Mustelidae*, the polecat has powerful scent glands. They smell so strongly that an old English name for the polecat is the *foumart*, or foul marten.

Ferrets, which as we have already seen (see page 14) are often domesticated and used on farms, are really a kind of polecat. Some are albino; others are coloured like the wild polecat. They are supposed to have descended not from our British wild polecat but from the *steppe polecat*, which lives in southern Russia and central Asia. However, many have escaped and interbred with wild polecats, so there is not much difference.

Ferrets become used to being handled by people but seldom become really tame. They need to be looked after with care and do not get friendly with their owner.

The martens are *Mustelidae* that live mostly in trees. The British example is the *pine marten*, which is sometimes said to be Britain's rarest animal. Once it was found in most of the forest and mountain districts of the British

The pine marten lives in tree holes, nest boxes and the nests of large birds and squirrels.

Isles, but shooting and trapping have exterminated it in all except some hilly regions of Wales, northern Scotland, north-west England and Ireland. But now they have stopped getting fewer in number, and the pine marten is increasing again and spreading further over country.

Although the pine marten is sometimes known as the

As well as small mammals and birds, pine martens eat insects, berries, fruit and beech mast.

tree weasel it is about the size of a polecat, or even larger. Its average length is nearly 2 feet 6 inches, which includes six or eight inches of bushy tail. It is reddish-brown, tinged with grey, with its face, feet, underparts and tail darker than the rest. It has a cream-coloured throat and chest. Its nose is longer and more pointed than the stoat's or polecat's. Its ears are larger, and so are its eyes.

Because it lives in trees most of the time, pine martens have long sharp claws, so that they can cling to tree trunks. The soles of their feet are covered with hair. They use their tails, which are almost as bushy as a squirrel's, for balancing.

Pine martens can climb and leap among the tree branches as nimbly as squirrels, which are their chief food. They also rob birds' nests and catch adult birds. But they are just as at home on the ground. They are even said to be able to catch a roe deer in fair chase. Rabbits, rats, mice and even hares are all prey to the pine marten. It will attack young lambs, and it plays havoc in the hen house. It can swim almost as well as an otter. Besides all of which, it will raid bee hives to get at the honey. And it loves ripe berries, like bilberries, raspberries and strawberries.

Unlike the polecat, the pine marten hunts chiefly by day. It is a solitary animal and likes hunting on its own. When sleeping it lies up in a hollow tree, or in a cranny among some rocks, or sometimes even the nest of a large bird, such as a crow or magpie.

51

A marten trapped in the snow. Its fur is extremely soft and very valuable.

The female marten makes her nest in places like this. She gets it ready by lining it with soft grass. Mating takes place in July or August, but the young do not start to grow in their mother's body until towards the end of winter. They are generally born in April, three to six in a litter. We do not know much about how they are brought up, but it seems that the young martens leave their den when they are about two months old. As with most other *Mustelidae*, they stay with their mother for a time, learning how to hunt.

We shall be extremely lucky if we ever see a wild marten in Britain. Several centuries ago, however, it was common and was hunted, both for sport and for its fur. Although fully grown pine martens are fierce and untameable, young ones are easily tamed, and people say that you can make attractive pets out of them.

Beech martens live all over Europe and Asia except the British Isles and Scandinavia. They are also called stone martens, *because they like rocky places.*

The name *pine* marten is misleading, for the animal lives in many sorts of trees and not only in pine woods. It may have been called that so as not to confuse it with the *beech marten*, which is found in most parts of Europe, though not in the British Isles. It is rather smaller than the pine marten, and its throat and chest are pure white, not cream-coloured.

The habits of the beech marten are very like those of the pine marten, except that it is not nearly as shy. In many European countries they make their homes around farmsteads and raid hen houses, pigeon lofts and beehives, like the pine marten. In ancient Greece they were tamed and kept in houses for killing mice.

Four other kinds of marten live in the northern forests of Europe, Asia and America. The *American marten* is very like the pine marten but, like many other animals which live in cold, northern climates, it has a very thick winter coat and so is hunted and trapped for its fur. The same is true of the *Siberian marten*, or *sable*, which has such a magnificent fur coat that it has been hunted until there are almost none left.

The largest of all the martens is the *fisher*, or *pecan*, which lives in North America. It is a magnificent animal, between three and four feet long. Its fur is dark brown, almost black, and very thick in winter. It does not catch fish but is an *arboreal* animal, catching squirrels and birds in the tree-tops like the other martens.

54

Opposite: *Beech martens have greyer coats than pine martens and a pure white bib, forked at the bottom.*

A wild American mink. Mink are savage killers, about two feet long, and weigh up to three pounds.

7: Mink and Skunks

Until recently there were mink in Europe and America, but none in Britain. The mink now found wild in Britain are *North American mink*, which have escaped from fur farms and are now breeding in the wild. There is also a *European mink*, which is not found in Britain.

Unlike the martens, mink do not live in tree tops. They like woods and can climb, but mainly they are fond of water. In the wild they live by streams and in marshes, and that is the sort of country they head for when they escape. The first ones that broke out in England made themselves at home by the river Teign in Devon, where they still live. That was about 1930, and since then there have been other escapes in many parts of England. In some regions wild mink are now quite common and are regarded as a serious pest.

Mink live chiefly on food that they can catch in the water. That, of course, includes fish, water birds, frogs, and water insects. However, like all the *Mustelidae*, they are savage killers and will attack almost anything. They will also kill far more than they need to eat. A mink in a

American mink were brought to Europe to make fur farms, but many escaped and now live wild. They prefer boggy and watery places to live in.

hen house goes mad with blood-lust and will kill as many hens as it can. It will even tackle such large birds as swans. And naturally it is very unpopular on rivers where fish, especially trout, are strictly preserved. Although people are trying to keep them down, however, mink manage to survive and increase in numbers.

Wild mink have dark brown coats with white throats. On fur farms mink with coats of a wide range of colours, from black to silver, pink and white, have been bred.

A pair of young European mink. They have white upper lips, unlike their American cousins.

These furs are very valuable, and rich people pay a lot of money to wear coats made from them. Wild mink are about eighteen inches long, with tails six inches long, but on fur farms they can be much larger. The male is nearly twice as big as the female.

Usually mink have one litter a year, of from four to ten kittens, which are born in March or April. The nest is usually a hole in a river bank, often under the roots of a tree. The gestation period is from six to twelve weeks, and

Like polecats, skunks have bright markings to warn other animals to keep away. This is called **defensive coloration.**

Baby skunks rest in a nest of leaves.

the young, as with other *Mustelidae*, are born blind and naked; they do not open their eyes until they are nearly a month old. The father mink sometimes helps the mother with the rearing and education of the kittens.

The *striped skunk* of North America is a handsome but very unpopular animal. It is about the size of a cat, and as it stands higher off the ground than most of the *Mustelidae*

61

Two skunks battle back to back, tail to tail. The one on the left is trying to push

63

er one off a morsel of food it has found, and turns round to see if it's winning.

it looks rather like one. But it has the small, flat head and pointed nose of the rest of its tribe.

The skunk has two fur coats, the outer one being long and harsh, the under coat soft and thick. It has a fine bushy tail, which it holds up in the air, like a waving banner. Its coat is mostly black, with white marks on its head and neck and a wide white stripe along the sides of its body.

Its unpopularity arises from the way it defends itself. Like stoats, weasels and other *Mustelidae*, it has two glands beneath its tail, but the fluid in them has a far worse smell than any of the other animals. It can be squirted for a foot or more. If you get in the way of it, it burns your skin and can cause temporary blindness if it gets in your eyes. You can smell a skunk half a mile away, and the scent lingers for days.

Luckily the skunk gives some warning before using this weapon. First, when threatened, it stamps its feet on the ground. Then it raises its tail, with the tip hanging down. Finally, when it lifts the tip of its tail – then beware!

Confident that they can defend themselves, skunks trot along public roads and paths quite openly, though usually at night, for they are nocturnal animals. In the United States and Canada you can often meet a family party on the road, the young prancing about behind their parents. Since there are now such a lot of cars on the road, this fearlessness has done them no good.

In America and Canada people think of skunks with

mixed feelings. They are valued because of the huge numbers of mice and rats that they kill. On the other hand they also kill poultry and take eggs. Their fur, too, is quite valuable, and skunk fur farms have been started. Skunks are easily tamed and make interesting pets. They will not use their scent defences against people they know.

The breeding habits of the skunk are like the other *Mustelidae*. The young are born in late spring or early summer; there are from four to ten in a litter; and their eyes open at the end of about three weeks.

There are several other sorts of skunk in North America, but they are mainly different from striped skunks in their markings. Skunks very like them are also found in South America.

Skunks are so confident, with their powerful scent glands and defensive coloration, that they do not have most animals' fear of man.

The wolverine: the largest and fiercest of the Mustelidae.

8: Other Cousins

The giant of the stoat and weasel world is the *wolverine*. It is a truly fearsome creature, more than four feet long and standing eighteen inches high. An adult wolverine weighs as much as 36 pounds. It has short, powerful legs and a thickset body. Its coat is thick and shaggy and its tail bushy.

While other *Mustelidae* rely on agility and speed to catch their prey, the wolverine charges ahead like a bulldozer or heavy truck. Compared to stoats and weasels it is slow and cumbersome. But it has all the ferocity and bloodthirstiness of the rest of the tribe. Another name for it is the *glutton*, because it is so greedy.

The wolverine hunts alone, not in a pack, and is nocturnal. If, plodding through the northern forest, one comes upon a wolf, bear or puma standing over an animal it has just killed, it does not hesitate. It charges straight in and tries to drive the killer away. So fierce is it that often the wolf or bear, although it may be much bigger than its attacker, retreats and leaves the carcase to it.

Wolverines live in Asia and North America, and in the very north of Europe. A wolverine can live as long as 18 years, but they are often shot for the damage they do.

Wolverines kill deer three or four times their own size. Sometimes they lie in ambush on tree branches and drop on the deer as they pass. They are also very fond of beavers, which they catch by breaking into their lodges in frozen lakes and rivers. They dig out mice and other small animals, and will also eat carrion. Trappers hate wolverines because they kill and eat the animals caught in their traps. They gulp down their food in great lumps, and are said to eat more, for their size, than any other carnivorous animal. When they have eaten all they can, they make stores of what is left over, for future use. They do this especially with large birds like grouse.

Although the wolverine is found in the northern parts of the United States, it is mainly an Arctic animal. It lives in fir forests and out on the tundra of northern Europe and Asia as well as in Canada and Alaska. Its thick fur, which is a protection against the cold, is valuable; but more often, however, it is killed because of its savagery and the damage it causes. It must be very hard to love a wolverine. If they were as large as lions they would be the most terrible animals alive.

As we have already noticed, many of the tropical *Mustelidae* are *arboreal*, that is, they live in trees. The *tayra* is a dark brown animal very like a stoat which lives in the forests of South and Central America. It is considerably larger than a stoat, up to three or four feet long, and is extremely fierce. Although it mostly feeds on rats, mice,

A European mink in the snow. Notice its white lower lip.

birds and even insects, it sometimes kills small deer. It often hunts in packs.

In the tropical grassland of Africa live two little animals which look very like each other. One is the *striped weasel*; the other, a stoat-like animal with the pleasant name *zorilla*. Both are striped black-and-white, like a skunk. Naturalists say this is *warning coloration*, which tells other animals that they are dangerous. Both can squirt a foul-smelling fluid at their enemies, just like skunks.

On the grasslands of South America lives another stoat-like animal, the *lesser grison*, or *huron*, which has a rather attractive habit. In order to see over the top of the tall grass it often stands on its hind legs, like a sentinel. It then stands about two feet high, and little heads of grisons can be seen bobbing up over the sea of grass on the Argentinian prairies.

We find we have mixed feelings about the *Mustelidae*. We like their playfulness, agility and incredible energy (apart from the slow wolverine); but on the other hand, they are insatiable butchers, the terror of all other small creatures of the countryside. People who live in the country are pleased when they kill mice and rats but angry when they kill poultry and pheasants. Whatever we think, the stoats and weasels carry on with their campaign of carnage, caring for nothing except their next meal.

Opposite: *An American stoat or short-tailed weasel.*

Glossary

ALBINO. A colour variation in animals, when they have white fur or hair and pink eyes.

ARBOREAL. Living in trees.

BERSERK. When an animal goes berserk it is filled with a fierce battle fury which compels it to kill and keep on killing.

BURROWS. Tunnels in the ground, dug by animals.

CAMOUFLAGE. Concealment by blending with one's background. It is usually achieved in nature by a colour pattern which breaks up the outline of the animal as well as matching the background. The animal should also remain perfectly still.

CARNAGE. Bloodshed and death on a large scale.

CARNIVOROUS. Flesh-eating.

CARRION. Dead and decaying flesh.

CUMBERSOME. Heavily clumsy.

DELAYED IMPLANTATION. A process by which, after mating, the fertilized eggs remain within their mother's body for long periods without growing. In some animals of the stoat family mating takes place in spring or summer but the eggs do not start to grow into young animals until the following spring.

ERMINE. Another name for the stoat, but especially used for the stoat in its white winter coat.

GESTATION. The period between mating and the birth of the baby animal; the period during which the baby is carried in its mother's body. With *delayed implantation* the gestation period is reckoned from the time at which the egg starts to develop, not from the time of mating.

INSATIABLE. Impossible to satisfy.

KITTENS. Young stoats and weasels. Adult males are *dog* stoats. Adult females are *bitch* stoats.

LITTER. All the young born to a female at one time are known as a litter.

LODGES. The rather elaborate houses built by beavers, of twigs and leaves, half in and half out of the water.

MUSTELIDAE. The scientific name given to the family to which belong all the animals dealt with in this book, as well as the otter and badger.

MYXOMATOSIS. A deadly disease which killed off vast numbers of rabbits in the 1950s.

NOCTURNAL. Active mainly at night.

PLAY. Play in animals is not only an outlet for high spirits but a preparation for the business of adult life. By playing, carnivorous animals, such as stoats and weasels, learn how to stalk, pounce on and grapple with their prey.

RODENTS. A group of animals which have two pairs of long and sharp front teeth, especially suited for gnawing. Rats, mice and squirrels are rodents.

TALONS. The sharp, curved claws of birds of prey.

TERRITORY. An area of land regarded by an animal as its own property. Animals will often drive away from their territory other animals of the same species, which they regard as rivals.

TUNDRA. The barren Arctic regions of north America, Europe and Asia.

Finding Out More

We may see stoats and weasels anywhere in Britain, though weasels are not found in Ireland. Going to look for them is of not much use, as they roam about the countryside and may turn up anywhere. But you are more likely to see them on farmland than in the wilder parts of the country.

We shall be very lucky if we manage to see polecats and pine martens wild in Britain. Polecats we might see by night in marshy or mountain districts in the wilder parts of Wales; pine martens in forests on the mountains of Wales, northern England and Scotland. You may see mink near rivers in Devon, Hampshire and a few other counties.

There are, however, fairly numerous mink farms in different parts of the United Kingdom. And on farms we may sometimes see domesticated ferrets in their cages. They are really a kind of polecat.

The other *Mustelidae* mentioned in this book may be seen in the Small Mammal House of most zoos.

Books to read:

British Mammals by L. Harrison Matthews (Collins).

Systematic Dictionary of Mammals of the World by Maurice Burton (Museum Press).

The Oxford Book of Vertebrates by Marion Nixon (Oxford University Press).

The Living World of Animals (Readers Digest Association).

The Book of the British Countryside (Automobile Association).

Mammals of Britain: Their Tracks, Trails and Signs by M. J. Lawrence and R. W. Brown (Blandford).

Animal Life of the British Isles by Edward Step (Warne).

Zoo in the Garden by Jeremy Lingard (Dent).

Picture Credits

The publishers thank the following for permission to use their pictures: Pictorial Press Ltd, *frontispiece*, p. 37; Mary Evans Picture Library, *title page*, p. 76; Frank W. Lane, pp. 6, 10, 14, 16, 22, 23, 28, 33, 35, 42, 44, 50, 53, 61, 62–3, 65, 66, 68–9, 72; Bruce Coleman Ltd, pp. 8, 9, 13, 20, 21, 25, 26, 27, 31, 32, 34, 36, 38, 41, 45, 46, 55, 58, 59, 60; Zoological Society of London, pp. 12, 17; Natural History Photographic Agency, pp. 15, 18, 30; Ardea Photographics, pp. 56, 71.